Publish and be DAMNED!

Publish and be DAMNED!

Cartoons for International PEN

EDITED BY MARK BRYANT

HEINEMANN KINGSWOOD

All the cartoons in this book were donated for a special
auction conducted by Bonhams in November 1988 and
all royalties from sales of the book and all the proceeds
of the auction go to International PEN to help writers
in prison worldwide.

Thanks are due to all those cartoonists whose generos-
ity has made this book and the auction possible and to
the editors of the various newspapers and magazines
in which some of the cartoons first appeared. Special
thanks also go to Tim Heald, Lady Antonia Fraser
and Siobhan Dowd of International PEN's Writers
in Prison Committee; Derek Wyatt and Margot
Richardson of Heinemann Kingswood, for all their
help.

M.B.

Heinemann Kingswood
Michelin House, 81 Fulham Road,
London SW3 6RB

LONDON   MELBOURNE   AUCKLAND

Cartoons © 1988 International PEN
Foreword © 1988 Tom Stoppard

First published 1988

ISBN 0 434 98155 9

Typeset by Rowland Phototypesetting Ltd,
Bury St Edmunds, Suffolk
Printed in Great Britain by Redwood Burn Ltd,
Trowbridge, Wiltshire

Acknowledgements

For their kind permission to use the cartoons in this book, International PEN and the publishers would like to thank the following:

City Limits
Daily Express
Daily Telegraph
Field Newspaper Syndicate
Guardian
Knight Features
The Listener
Private Eye
Publishing News
Punch
Sunday Express
The Times

Also Mrs Marjorie Watts for donating the Arthur Watts cartoon and Michael Meyer and Routledge & Kegan Paul for the use of 'Europe's Prisoners' by Sidney Keyes from *The Collected Poems of Sidney Keyes* edited by Michael Meyer.

Europe's Prisoners

Never a day, never a day passes
But I remember them, their stoneblind faces
Beaten by arclights, their eyes turned inward
Seeking an answer and their passage homeward.

For being citizens of time, they never
Would learn the body's nationality.
Tortured for years now, they refuse to sever
Spirit from flesh or accept our callow century.

. . .

Whatever days, whatever seasons pass,
The prisoners must stare in pain's white face:
Until at last the courage they have learned
Shall burst the walls and overturn the world.

Sidney Keyes

Foreword

A chunk of type attached to a collection of cartoons? It sounds like the original lead balloon, but bear with it. How many books stop to thank you for the money and tell you who's getting it?

PEN stands for Poets, Essayists and Novelists, for the sake of the acronym; in the other sense it stands for every kind of writer. WiPC stands for Writers in Prison Committee. During a previous PEN effort to raise funds for the cause, an enthusiastic donor whipped out his chequebook with the cry, 'Writers in prison? Capital idea! Best place for them!' So a few words of explanation may not be amiss.

The idea that writers should stand up for each other in times of oppression was implicit in PEN's constitution from the beginning (1921), but those were comparatively innocent days. PEN was a writers' club and it is doubtful that the founding members imagined a time when much of the club's business would be concerned with writers behind bars. In the 1930s there were cases which became *causes celèbres* (PEN was in the forefront of the campaign to release Arthur Koestler, imprisoned and condemned to death in Spain in 1937) but such is the progress of the twentieth century that in the post-war years the club, now International PEN, was confronted with the systematic persecution of writers left, right and centre, and indeed Left, Right and Centre. PEN itself makes no political distinctions between the hundreds of writers who are in prison, or between the governments who put them there. The concern is simply that men and women are being locked away because their writing is offensive or inconvenient to those who govern them. By 1960 it became necessary to form a special committee to deal exclusively with bringing aid, and if possible liberty, to imprisoned writers. It was an exiled Hungarian writer living in England who first proposed such a committee a year before the founding of Amnesty International (which exists to help all 'prisoners of conscience', not writers specifically).

The money from this book will go to pay for legal defences, for medicines, for the support of prisoners' families, for telegrams (a PEN telegram to a head of state costs an average of £40) and for the services of a small under-paid staff. The Writers in Prison Committee is indebted to the publishers, to the artists and to you the purchaser. 'Without good friends like you,' wrote one of PEN's adopted prisoners in 1984, 'I don't think I would have the strength to carry this heavy chain of my incarceration.'

So much for my introduction, and I wish I could have drawn it. The gift of caricature and cartoon is one I have always envied, and one which has given me endless delight. To the pens which follow mine, I take my writer's hat off.

Tom Stoppard
December 1987

"Dear Diary. Stayed in again today . . ."

LISTEN, HARRY. GREAT
GRAFFITI DOESN'T HAPPEN
WITHOUT A STUGGLE.

"Right then, whose turn for the book this week?"

"A limited edition? I saw it as a well-thumbed, dog-eared paperback."

"Him? He's my publisher."

"I get five years now and then another five years when the book's completed."

"No sir, they ain't h'alphabetical. They is tallest on the right, shortest on the left."

"Quick, Gordon – it's the film of your next book!"

"I'm glad we finally managed to find a use for all those unpublished
manuscripts of yours."

"Just six weeks a member of the Writers' Circle and already I've been
elected to the committee!"

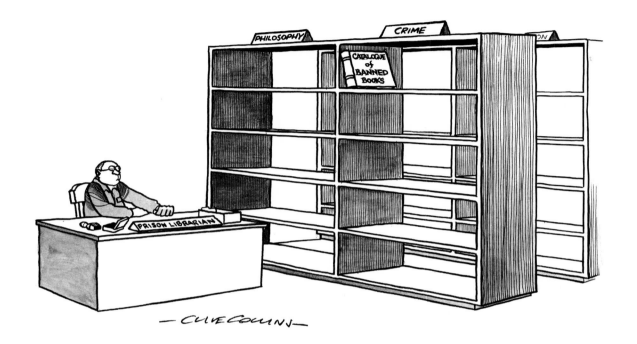

"It's no good, Martha – I *still* don't feel inspired to write."

"Jeremy's book is doing quite nicely, although we had rather hoped
he would have been plagiarised by now."

"He's having lunch with his agent."

"How do you know the chapters will get there in the right order?"

Yes but...

I DESPERATELY WANT TO WRITE A HUGELY SUCCESSFUL BLOCKBUSTER !!

I WANT TO BE ABLE TO SAY, "**YES**! I **WILL** BE A **TAX-EXILE!**"....

OR....

"**NO**! I WILL **NOT** BE A **TAX-EXILE!**"

I DESPERATELY WANT TO BE IN THE POSITION OF **HAVING** TO MAKE SUCH AN AGONISING **CHOICE!**

I'M BASHING OUT FIVE THOUSAND WORDS **EACH DAY!**

BUT THERE **ARE** PROBLEMS.

MY GIRLFRIEND, FOR EXAMPLE.

SHE **WILL** KEEP PEERING OVER MY SHOULDER.

I WAS WRITING THIS CHAPTER ABOUT THESE **WHITE-SLAVE TRADERS** SUBJECTING MY **INNOCENT HEROINE** TO THEIR **UNSPEAKABLE LUSTS!**

"THAT'S **VERY** GOOD! SAID MY GIRLFRIEN "THAT'S **VERY** FUNNY

"IT'S **NOT MEANT** TO BE **FUNNY!**" I CRIED "THERE'S **NO SUCH THING** AS A **COMIC** BLOCKBUSTER.

BLOCKBUSTERS ARE LONG, TURGID, MELODRAMAS **TOTALLY DEVOID OF HUMOUR.**

MY BOOK IS **TOTALL DEVOID OF HUMOUR**

"IT'S NOT ONLY VERY FUNNY," SHE PERSISTED.....

"IT'S ALSO RATHER **SWEET**!"

"**SWEET**!" I SHRIEKED. "WHAT DO YOU **MEAN**, 'IT'S RATHER SWEET'?"

"WELL, IT **IS**," SHE SAID. "ALL THOSE **WICKED** SLAVE TRADERS PULLING AT THAT LITTLE PRIG'S CHEMISE — AND SNIGGERING. IT'S ALL SO DELIGHTFULLY **VICTORIAN**."

"**YOU** COULD DO **BETTER**, I SUPPOSE!?" I SAID.

"**YES**!" SHE REPLIED SCORNFULLY, REACHING FOR HER BALL-POINT.

"WHAT'S MORE, **MY** BOOK WILL BE **VERY NINETEEN-EIGHTIES RAUNCHY INDEED!**"

I **BELIEVE** HER!

IF HER BOOK IS A SUCCESS **SHE** MIGHT BECOME A **TAX-EXILE**.

MAYBE SHE'LL TAKE **ME** WITH HER.

I HOPE SO! I'M **FOND** OF HAPPY ENDINGS!

Now! magazine 12.9.80. © JOHN JENSEN 1980

"Look up 'Hernia', mate – under 'H'."

"Here comes Chapter Nineteen."

"Ever thought about starting a bookshop?"

(The Government's attempt to suppress *Spycatcher*, the auto-biography of former MI5 'molecatcher' Peter Wright causes great controversy. *Ed.*)

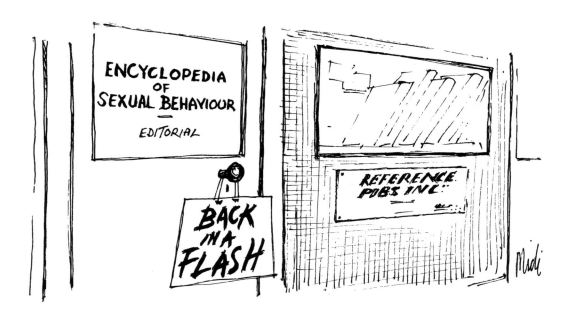

"I'm afraid this poetic licence has expired, sir."

(Peter Wright's autobiography, freely on sale in the USA, is banned
in Great Britain. None the less, many copies are circulated illegally.
Ed.)

"Richard is researching his new novel which is to be set in London's
mean streets."

AH- A SOUTH FACING LIGHT ...

DISG

"My dear Lord Longford! You've qualified to join us for a cup
of tea!"

(Lord Longford's campaign for the release of long-incarcerated
Moors murderer, Myra Hindley, causes much comment. Militant
Labour councillors Derek Hatton (Liverpool) and Bernie Grant
(Brent) welcome him to the 'Loony Left'. Headmistress Maureen
McGoldrick, accused of racist attitudes, is dunked in the teapot. *Ed.*)

"Philip Larkin? For one minute I thought someone else shared my
opinion of the Poet Laureate."

(The public reception of a commemorative poem by a recently
elected Poet Laureate, Ted Hughes, is decidedly lukewarm. *Ed.*)

"All right, you can put up my next MS, but I'm not bloody going
around in a floral print."

(The Betty Trask Award for a 'romantic or other novel of a traditional
rather than experimental nature' is inaugurated. Administered by
the Society of Authors, it becomes the British book trade's richest
annual prize at £40,000. *Ed.*)

"Colin says he can spare fifteen minutes to enjoy your company
before he starts his next novel."

"I don't know why you're moaning, you writers are supposed to
work better under pressure!"

"Withhold the front page!"

"I'm in here for petty larceny but they have this thing about
throwing away the key."

"And if you pay £15 now, this will entitle you to write out further cheques at regular intervals of three months."

"For future reference Miss Crimp, the phrase is 'shop soiled'."

"It's quite fair and simple – a white cross for the Whites, and a black
cross for the Blacks."

(During the presidential elections in South Africa, former premier
P. W. Botha insists that balloting has been conducted in a fully
democratic way. *Ed.*)

The rain it raineth on the just
  And also on the unjust fella;
But chiefly on the just because
  The unjust steals the just's umbrella.

Charles Bowen

"Don't worry, we'll have you out of here in no time."

"Since the Bishop of Durham threw out the map, we've lost the way
for some unknown reason."

(When the Bishop of Durham makes a statement casting doubt on
the historical accuracy of parts of the Bible, the Church of England,
with Dr Robert Runcie at its head as Archbishop of Canterbury, is
thrown into considerable disarray. *Ed.*)

"You're lucky – my last return from Public Lending Right said I owe *them* money."

"Doesn't everyone have a fancy-dress cupboard?"

(Erstwhile UN General Secretary, Kurt Waldheim, is accused of possible war crimes when he announces his candidacy for the post of Austrian premier. *Ed.*)

"He was a mediocre painter, but a truly great drunk."

(A portrait of Czech author, Franz Kafka, looms behind Alan
Bennett's writing desk. From a review of Bennett's play, *The
Insurance Man*, in *The Listener*. *Ed.*)

"I'm in for hanky panky."

There is one thing certain, namely,
that we can have nothing certain;
therefore it is not certain that we
can have nothing certain.
                              Samuel Butler

"Oh God! This could take for ever!"

"OK, so you did bite Barbara Woodhouse – I was neutered by James
Herriot."

(Illustration to correspondence in the letters page of the *Guardian* on the death of poet Philip Larkin. *Ed.*)

"Actually, no, it's *Eric* Hood. I rob everybody and keep the lot."

"I'm sorry, madam, but so would your signature gradually become illegible if you autographed as many books as Mr Archer."

THE GHOST (*as midnight strikes*): 'Same as ever: I never can get here
soon enough to hear anything but the last few bars of the Savoy
Band!'

(This fine cartoon by Arthur Watts (1883–1935) was kindly donated by his widow, Mrs Marjorie Watts, whose mother, Catherine Amy Dawson-Scott – better known as 'Mrs Sappho' – was the original founder of PEN. Remarkably, the cartoon was first published in the Christmas 1927 number of the *Sketch* [not a Walkman but an early radio]. *Ed.*)

"They just don't write them like that any more!"

(The German writer, polemicist and active PEN member, Günter Grass, from a review of his book *The Rat* published in *The Listener*. *Ed.*)

Contributing Cartoonists

STEVE BELL   b1951

Born in Walthamstow and educated at Slough Grammar School, Middlesbrough Art College and Leeds University, he taught art in a Birmingham secondary school until classroom phobia drove him to throw it all in and take up freelance cartooning. His first regular paid work was for *Whoopee!* comic in 1978. Then, via various magazines, newspapers and comics he began drawing strips for *City Limits*, the *Guardian* and recently the *New Statesman*. His work has been described as 'an almost obscene series of caricatures . . .' (House of Lords, March 1987).

NEIL BENNETT

Has just become a full-time cartoonist at the age of 46, having resigned from teaching English in a college of further education. He thinks the lunatic schemes of Messrs Joseph and Baker could better be implemented without him. He contributes to *Private Eye*, *Punch*, *New Statesman* and *The Cricketer*.

SIMON BOND   b1947

A course at the West Sussex College of Art and Design led to eight months on the dole before Simon found work in Nottingham as a paste-up artist on the *Tatler*, only to be sacked for illness.

After a period as a manager of a jewellery shop he took advantage of his dual citizenship to emigrate to America in 1970. Pursued various jobs until metamorphosing into a serious cartoonist in Phoenix, Arizona. The publication in 1981 of *101 Uses For A Dead Cat* brought him worldwide success and notoriety.

HECTOR BREEZE

Prefers to remain anonymous.

MEL CALMAN   b1931

Educated at Perse School Cambridge, St Martin's School of Art and Goldsmiths' College, Mel Calman has been a cartoonist on the *Daily Express* (1957–63), *Sunday Telegraph* (1964–65), *Observer* (1965–66), *Sunday Times* (1969–84) and has been working for *The Times* since 1979. He also runs The Cartoon Gallery – a gallery devoted to cartoon art he founded in 1970 – has produced an animated cartoon and has contributed illustrations to many books and periodicals. He lists his recreations as 'brooding and worrying'.

'CLUFF' – JOHN LONGSTAFF   b1949

After a graphics course, 'Cluff' worked in local government. He began cartooning six years ago and is now printed in *Private Eye, Punch* and *Literary Review*. When not working or busy bringing up his four-year-old daughter he enjoys walking in the Yorkshire Dales.

CLIVE COLLINS   b1942

Went to Kingston Art School, after which he worked in insurance, as a film extra, ran a film studio and repped for a small artwork studio, before becoming political cartoonist for the *Sunday People*. He is now deputy political cartoonist on the *Daily Mirror*, and regularly draws cartoons for *Punch* and *Playboy*. He was selected as Cartoonist of the Year by the Cartoonists Club of Great Britain in 1984 and 1985, and was President of the Salon Jury, to mention just a few of the accolades he has been awarded over the years.

MICHAEL CUMMINGS OBE

Son of A. J. Cummings, political editor of the *News Chronicle*, Michael Cummings studied art at the Chelsea School of Art and his first job was as a cartoonist on *Tribune* during Michael Foot's time as editor. He joined the *Daily Express* in 1949, added work for the *Sunday Express* in 1958 and has been working for both newspapers ever since. He also contributed to *Punch* during the years of Malcolm Muggeridge's editorship, and has had his work reproduced in many newspapers and journals worldwide.

FRANK DICKENS

Frank Dickens has been cartooning for 28 years and has won the Cartoonists Club of Great Britain Award four times. He is perhaps best known for his cartoon strips 'Bristow' and 'Albert Herbert Hawkins (The Naughtiest Boy in the World)'. His hobbies include cycling and theatregoing. He is at present working on a musical.

'DISH' – NEIL DISHINGTON

Born: a long time ago. Art school, teaching, illustrations, cartooning, mending the fence, bringing up children etc. Now over 50 but, like Tomi Ungerer, believes that all that he has done is 'merely an apprenticeship for what is to follow'.

JOHN DONEGAN   b1926

Came to illustration and cartooning via advertising.

RIANA DUNCAN   b1951

After attending Art School in Holland, she spent several years exhibiting graphics and textiles before turning to writing and illustrating children's books. Took up cartooning seven years ago and her work has appeared in *Punch*, the *Observer*, the *Guardian*, *Men Only*, *Weekend*, *She*, etc. Has now returned to writing and illustrating for children. Riana Duncan lives and works aboard a sailing yacht in Lymington.

BARRY FANTONI   b1940

A novelist, broadcaster, cartoonist and jazz musician. Has been on the editorial staff of *Private Eye* since 1963 and diary cartoonist of *The Times* since 1983. Studied at Camberwell School of Arts and Crafts. Has cartooned for *The Listener*, been art critic of *The Times* and has been a film and TV actor. His recreations are snooker, road running and animal welfare.

MICHAEL FFOLKES

Was born in London in 1925. A child of the Disney generation, his earliest drawings were of the Seven Dwarfs and Ferdinand the Bull. After a period at St Martin's School of Art he worked at various commercial art studios, spent three years in the Royal Navy and returned to study painting at the Chelsea School of Art before becoming a professional cartoonist. He has worked in advertising, book illustration, film credit titles and animation and his drawings have appeared in *Punch*, *Lilliput*, *Daily Telegraph*, *Sunday Telegraph*, *Playboy*, *Private Eye*, *New Yorker*, *Connoisseur*, *Reader's Digest* and the German journal *Pardon*, amongst others.

GEORGE GALE

Was born and educated in Scotland but has been living in London since the 1950s. After studying engineering and a period as a commercial artist he began freelancing, selling cartoons to *The Times*, *The Economist* and other

British and European newspapers and journals. He has been editorial cartoonist with the *Daily Telegraph* since 1986 and lives in Richmond with his wife, a teacher.

DAVID HALDANE

Lives in the north-east of England and is 33 years old. He has been a freelance cartoonist for ten years, contributing work to *Punch*, *Private Eye* and the *Daily Mirror*, and has recently done some scriptwriting for 'Spitting Image'.

DAVID HAWKER

Sold his first cartoon in 1967 when working as an architectural draughtsman and went full-time two years later, selling his first cartoon to *Punch* in 1970. He stopped cartooning briefly in 1976 to qualify as a driving instructor and still puts in some part-time hours behind the wheel. Though his work appears in various publications he mainly concentrates on *Punch*.

MICHAEL HEATH   b1935

Michael Heath was born in London and is a regular contributor to the *Sunday Times*, *New Standard* and the *Guardian* and for many years his cartoons have been the mainstay of *Punch* and *Private Eye*.

MARTIN HONEYSETT   b1943

Left Croydon School of Art after one year to take to the road. Spent six years abroad in various jobs – as a lumberjack and trucker in Canada – before returning to England in 1969. Began cartooning on his return whilst working as a bus driver for London Transport. Now a full-time cartoonist, appearing mainly in *Private Eye* and *Punch*.

TONY HUSBAND   b1950

Had no formal training as an artist but influenced by his father who dabbled in drawing and writing. Found work in the printing side of an advertising agency, as well as spells of window dressing and repairing jewellery. Four and a half years ago his first book of drawings *Use Your Head* was published, and he is now a regular contributor to *Private Eye* and *Punch*.

IAN JACKSON   b1964

Studied at Jacob Gramer College of Art, Leeds, and has been designing greetings cards since 1982 and cartooning regularly for *Punch* since 1984. He also works trotter-in-glove with Uncle Pigg for *Oink!* and occasionally draws cartoons for *Playboy*. When he is not doing any of the above he stuffs animals.

TIMOTHY JAQUES

Educated at Uppingham School, Timothy Jaques received a National Diploma in Design from the London School of Printing in 1957 and was a director of the Peter Hatch Partnership before becoming a freelance graphic designer in 1965. He is consultant designer to a number of companies including Nordic Bank, Longman, British Museum Publications and INSEAD Fontainebleau, has illustrated books by Jilly Cooper, Arthur Marshall, Douglas Sutherland and Gyles Brandreth amongst others, and has been a frequent contributor of cartoons to *Publishing News*.

JOHN JENSEN   b1930

John Jensen arrived in England in 1950 and spent three years drawing for the *Birmingham Gazette*, and another three for the *Glasgow Bulletin* before returning to London where he contributed to *Lilliput*, *Daily Express*, *Evening News* and *New Statesman*. He was a political cartoonist of the *Sunday Telegraph* for 19 years and also contributed theatre caricatures to the *Tatler* and social comment to the *Spectator*. He worked for *Now!* magazine during its short lifetime, and now draws regularly for *Punch*. He has illustrated more than 50 books and edited a volume of drawings by H. M. Bateman. Writes (anything but letters) when not drawing, draws when not writing. Sleeps when not doing either. He is married with two children.

'KAL' – KEVIN KALLAUGHER   b1955

Was born in Norwalk, Connecticut, USA. After graduating from Harvard University in 1977 he came to England on a bicycle tour. He joined *The Economist* in March 1978 and has been there ever since. He has been the political cartoonist for the *Observer* (1983–86), *Today* (1986–87) and currently for the *Sunday Telegraph*. His work is widely syndicated, appearing regularly in over 100 papers worldwide. He lives in Brighton with his wife, Sue, and children, Amy and Daniel.

DAVID LANGDON OBE

An ex-RAF squadron leader, David Langdon is a regular contributor to *Punch*, *New Yorker* and other publications and is a member of the *Punch* 'Table'. He has also illustrated books, including a series of humorous titles by George Mikes, and is official artist to the Centre Internationale Audio-Visuel. He is married with three children and lives in Hertfordshire.

'LARRY' – TERENCE PARKS   b1927

'Larry' has been a freelance artist since 1957, contributing mainly to *Punch* and *Private Eye*. For a few 'mad years' in the early 1970s he painted scenery for Joan Littlewood's Theatre Royal in London. Currently living in Stratford-on-Avon with his wife, 'Larry' has a grown-up son and daughter. He is a great country lover, particularly of the pubs therein, for which he advocates the return of old lino, fag ends and dogs, and the removal of pile carpets, flower arrangements and canned music.

PETER MADDOCKS   b1929

Was once told by a psychiatrist that he was 'a creative psychopath'. Boredom with drawing daffodils at Moseley School of Art led him to take off around the world. Returning at the age of 21, he set up his own advertising agency, designing cinema posters, moving on to produce his first cartoons for Fleet Street with the *Daily Sketch*. After periods with the *Daily Express*, *Standard* and *Evening News*, Maddocks went freelance. Not content with producing animated films for TV, he is also 'headmaster' of the London School of Cartooning.

'MARC' – MARK BOXER

Prefers to remain anonymous.

'MIDI' – MIKE DICKINSON   b1938

Mike Dickinson joined the book trade on leaving school and for the last twenty-five years he has been a publisher's representative. His cartoons first appeared in *Publishing News* in 1982 and he is now a regular weekly contributor. He has also written and illustrated several picture books for children.

JOHN MINNION   b1949

Is a regular political caricaturist for *New Statesman* (since 1978) and also draws a weekly music caricature in *The Listener*. His politics changed from pinky-red to muddy red-green mainly through reading Schumacher.

NICK NEWMAN   b1958

Nick Newman's drawing career began on his school-books. He read History at Oxford, worked on its notorious *Passing Wind* magazine, and has been a business journalist on *Management Today*. His favourite cartoonists include Honeysett, McLachlan and Austin, and he has concocted scripts for every edition of 'Spitting Image'. In his free time he works.

KEN PYNE   b1951

Started off as a layout artist on *Soap* and *Waste Reclamation and Disposal Weekly* before turning freelance, since when he's been taken up by *The Times*, *Private Eye*, *Punch* and others.

'RICHARD'

Prefers to remain anonymous.

LEN SPENCER

Prefers to remain anonymous.

BILL STOTT   b1944

Bill Stott was born in Preston, and studied painting and lithography at Harris College in his home town. His greatest influence has been Bill Tidy, and he carries a kidney donor card.

KEN TAYLOR

Coming from a background of commercial art and design, including UK and Canadian television, Ken Taylor is a Scottish cartoonist based in London. After seven years on the staff of the *Evening Standard* he turned freelance, producing daily strip cartoons for the *Daily Express* and the *Daily Star* simultaneously. A contributor to *Punch* for over twenty years he later became its design consultant and then Art Editor and is currently consultant to the *Daily* and *Sunday Express*.

ANNIE TEMPEST

Lives and works in London. Her cartoons have appeared in several national newspapers and she currently produces 'The Yuppies' strip cartoon for the *Daily Mail*. Her books include *How Green are Your Wellies?*, *Hooray Henry* and *Henry on Hols*.

GEOFF THOMPSON

Geoff Thompson is 33 and is married with three children. He works and sleeps in the bedroom of his thatched cottage near Yeovil. A redundancy casualty of the Westland affair, he took to professional cartooning in the autumn of 1986. His drawings have appeared in *Private Eye*, *Punch*, *New Statesman*, *Mayfair*, *Harper's*, *Men Only* and *Visitor* amongst others.

'VIC' – VIC GIBBONS

Grandson of the radical writer and co-founder of the Independent Labour Party, Joseph Burgess, Vic moved from his birthplace in Halifax to Chatham, Kent, in 1942 and attended Rochester Art School. During the Second World War he served on tanks in the 10th Royal Hussars and was for many years an industrial cartoonist at BP Oil's Kent Refinery before setting up his own design company, Vic Designs, at the age of 54. He has since retired, and his wife Rose says of him: 'He doesn't just draw cartoons, he *is* a cartoon!'

ARTHUR WATTS   b1883

Arthur Watts, who initiated the style of drawing from a height, using a lot of white space, studied art at the Slade in London. For his part in the Zeebrugge and Ostend raids while serving with the RNVR in the First World War he was awarded a DSO and bar. He was a regular contributor to *Punch* (from 1922), the *Sketch* and *Radio Times* (from 1928). He died in 1935.

MIKE WILLIAMS   b1940

Worked as an illustrator in a commercial art studio before becoming a freelance; now a regular contributor to *Punch*, *Private Eye* and *Playboy*.

Writers in Prison

Many people don't realise just how many writers and journalists are silenced for exercising their right to freedom of expression: some are in jail, others are confined in psychiatric hospitals, remote parts of their countries or even their own homes. PEN's Writers in Prison Committee has 340 names on its list, but the names below represent only the tip of the iceberg. Many other writers are banned, censored, deprived the means of making a living or suppressed in more subtle ways. Still others are so effectively silenced that organisations like PEN do not even know of their existence.

Writers and journalists (J) reported to be kidnapped, imprisoned, banned, under house or town arrest, or awaiting trial or disappeared, as at December 1987. Some have since been released – others have been arrested.

Afghanistan

Professor Habiburahman Hala

Angola

Horacio Martins Torrado

Central African Republic

Thomas Koazo

Chad

Saleh Gaba (J)

Chile

Juan Pablo Cardeñas
Gonzalo Toro Garland
Fernando Ortiz Letelier
Manuel Rivas Rachitoff (J)
Manuel Recabarren Rojas (J)
Diana Aaron Svigilsky (J)

China

Chen Erjin
He Qiu
Liu De
Liu Qing
Qin Yongmin
Xu Shuiliang
Xu Wenli
Xue Deyun
Yang Jing (J)
Wang Rongqing
Wang Xizhe
Wei Jingsheng
Zhang Jingsheng
Zhu Jianbin

Cuba

Gustavo Arcos Bergnes
Amado Rodriguez Fernandez
Alberto Fibla Gonzalez
Ariel Hidalgo
Angel Pardo Mazorra
Antonio Lopez Muniz
Alberto Jane Padron
Guillermo Rivas Porta (J)
Ernesto Diaz Rodriguez (J)
Luis Rodriguez Rodriguez (J)
Alberto Grau Sierra
Juan Alberto Valdes Teran
Manuel Marquez Trillo
Ignacio Cuesta Valle
Jesus Castro Villalonga

Czechoslovakia

Herman Chromy
Ervin Motl
Jiri Wolf

Egypt

Mohamed Moro

El Salvador

Amadeo Mendizabel (J)
Cesar Najarro (J)
Jaime Suarez Quemain (J)
Rene Tamsen
Edgar Mauricio Vallejo (J)

Ethiopia

Martha Kumsa
Bealu Girma

Ghana

Yao Graham (J)
Kwame Karikari (J)
Kwesi Pratt (J)
Ben Ephson

Guatemala

Abner Recinos Alfaro
Nicholas Blake (J)
Angel Claudio Calderon
Oscar Leonel Cordova
Sonia Calderon de Martell
Alaide Foppa de Solorzano
Valentin Ferrat (J)
Irma Flaquer (J)
Rolando Medina
Rodrigo Ramirez Morales
Manuel Rene Polanco Salguero

Indonesia

Pramoedya Ananta Toer

Israel

Khalil Achour
Mamoun al-Sayyid
Radwan Abu Ayyash
Nabhan Kreisheh
Mahmoud Ramahi

Jordan

Mazin 'Abd al'Wahid al-As'ad

Kenya

James Achira
Paul Amina (J)
John Baptista Kariamati
Ngotho wa Kariuki
Maina wa Kinyatti
Katama Mkangi (J)
Njuguna (Joseph) Mutahi
Wahome Mutahi

Dick Namadoa (J)
Mukaru Ng'ang'a
Odhiambo Okite (J)
Mugo Theuri Wanderi (J)

Lebanon

Terry Anderson (J)
William Buckley (J)
Alec Collett (J)
John MacCarthy (J)

Libya

Abdullah Salih Al Awami
Mostafa El Hashmi Ba'yu
Ramadan Ali Al Farisi
Ahmed Muhammad El Fitouri (J)
Khalifa Sifaw Khaboush
Omar Belgassem Shelig El Kikli
Jum'a Omar Bou Kleib
Sa'ad El Sawi Mahmoud
Muhammad Abdulhamid Al Maliki
Idris Juma' El Mismari
Fathi Nasib Muhammad
Ali Muhammad Hadidan Al Rheibi (J)
Muhammad Muhammad El Fgih Salih
Muhammad Omar Ben Saud
Abdessalam Muhammad Shehab
Idris Muhammad Ibn Tayeb

Malawi

Jack Mapanje

Malaysia

Syed Jaafar Alsagoff (J)
Ahman Sebi Abu Bakar
Dr Chandra Muzaffar

Mauritania

Tene Youssouf Gueye
Ibrahim Sarr (J)

Mexico

Jorge Enrique Hernandez Aguilar (J)
Israel Gutierrez Hernandez (J)
Juan Valdez Peña

Morocco

Abdelkader Chaoui
Ali Idrissi Kaitouni
Abraham Serfaty

Nepal

Birodh Khatiwada (J)
Chandralal Jah (J)
Dorje Lama (J)
Raghu Pant
Bhairav Risal (J)
Padam Thakurathi
Harihar Virahi

Peru

Jaime Ayala Sulca (J)

Romania

Nicolae Stoia

Singapore

Chia Thye Poh

South Africa

Mxolisi Jackson Fuzile (J)
Mbulelo Grootboom (J)
Mzayifani Hoffman (J)
Themba Khumalo
Mudini Maiva
Marapodi Mapalakanye
Vincent Mfundisi
Phyla Ngqumba (J)
Robert Tendamudzimo Ratshitanga
Jaki Seroke
Zwelakhe Sisulu (J)
William Smith
Brian Sokutu (J)
Moffat Zunga (J)

South Korea

Chang Ki-pyo
Kim Hyon-jang
Kim Nam-ju
Kim Sang-bok
Kim Yong-ho
Koh Kyong-dae
Koh Song-quk
Kung Uk-dong

Lee Pom
Lee Pu-yong
Lee Tae-bok
Park Chong-kyu
Yun Ho-dok

Syria

Samir al-Hassan
Ali al-Kurdi
'Izzat al-Mahmud (J)
Ali al-Rifa' i
Mazin al-Tu'mari
Nabil Bashir
Khalil Brayez
Rida Haddad (J)
Marwan Hamawi (J)
Muhammad Kutayla
'Imad Naddaf (J)
Jamal Rabi' (J)
Wa'il Sawwah
Tadrus Trad

Taiwan

Chang Hua-min
Shih Ming-teh

Tanzania

James Mapalala (J)
Mwinyi Juma Othman Upindo (J)

Tunisia

Rachid Ghannouchi

Turkey

Nevzat Acan
Fuat Akyurek
Ibrahim Arik
Irfan Asik (J)
Guzel Aslander
Oral Calislar
Mehmet Cerit
Mehmet Coban (J)
Mustafa Colak
Servet Ziya Corakli
Mete Dalgin (J)
Ilker Demir
Mustafa Dum (J)
Mustafa Eker (J)
Bektas Erdogan

Ersin Ergun
Fettah Erkan
Yasar Kaplan
Bayram Kazakli
Mustafa Kocak
Recep Marasli
Mehmet Ozgen (J)
Candemir Ozler
Feyzullah Ozer (J)
Ali Rabus
Alaattin Sahin (J)
Orhan Selen
Emine Senlikoglu
Osman Tas
Erhan Tuskan
Huseyin Ulger
Hasran Fikret Ulusoydan
Ali Haydar Yildirim (J)
Mustafa Yildirimturk (J)
Veli Yilmaz

Uganda

Anthony Ssekweyama (J)

Union of the Soviet Socialist Republics (divided according to Republics)

ESTONIA
Mart Niklus

GEORGIA
Vazha Zhgenti

LATVIA
Gunars Astra
Zanis Skudra

LITHUANIA
Balys Gajauskas
Gintautas Iesmantas
Viktoras Petkus

RUSSIA
Vladimir Rusak
Polynek Vasily Semyonivich
Vladimir Vasiliev
Tatyana Velikanova
Viktor Zinoviev

UKRAINE
Yury Badyzo
Mykola Horbal
Pavel Kampov
Mykola Krainik
Dmitri Kvetsko

Levko Lukyanenko
Vasily Ovsienko
Semyon Skalich
Ivan Sokulsky

Venezuela

Carlos Perez Baez
Victor Gonzalez (J)

Vietnam

Anh Thuan
Bui Ngoc Dung
Cao Thoai Chau
Dang Tran Huan
Dang Tran Lan
Doan Ke Tuong (J)
Doan Quoc Sy
(Thich) Duc Nhuan
Duong Dien Nghi
Duong Hung Cuong
Ho Van Dong (J)
Hoang Hai Thuy

Khuat Duy Trac
Le Khiem
Le Van Tien
Mai Duc Khoi (J)
Nguyen Bao Danh
Nguyen Chi Thien
Nguyen Hai Chi
Nguyen Khanh Giu
Nguyen Kim Tuan
Nguyen Ngoc Tan (J)
Nguyen Thanh Nhan
Nguyen thi Phuoc Ly
Nguyen Tu
Nguyen Van Khanh
Nguyen Van Than
Pham Dai
Pham Gia Tien
Phan Nhat Nam (J)
Phan The Hung
To Huy Co (J)
Tran Duc Uyen
Trinh Viet Thanh (J)
Truong Vi Tri (J)
(Thich) Tue Sy

Phan Van Lam Binh
Tran Buu Khanh
Tran Dai
Tran Dai Long (J)
Tran Dinh Tuyen
Tran Duy Hinh
Tran Minh Dung
Tran Quy Phong (J)
Tran Tu Binh
Vo Long Te
Vo Long Trieu
Vu Duc Hai (J)
Vu Duc Nghiem (J)
Vu Van Anh (J)

Yugoslavia

Dragan Bogdanovski
Vjenceslav Cizek
Adem Demaci
Alija Isetbegovic
Miodrag Milic
Rrahim Sadiku (J)
Melike Salibegovic

International PEN has centres in the following countries: Argentina, Australia, Austria, Bangladesh, Belgium, Brazil, Bulgaria, Canada, Chile, China, Colombia, Cote d'Ivoire, Cyprus, Czechoslovakia, Denmark, Egypt, Estonia, Federal Republic of Germany, Finland, France, German Democratic Republic, Great Britain, Greece, Guatemala, Hong Kong, Hungary, Iceland, India, Indonesia, Ireland, Israel, Italy, Japan, Jordan, Korea, Latvia, Lebanon, Liechtenstein, Mexico, Monaco, Netherlands, New Zealand, Nicaragua, Norway, Pakistan, Paraguay, Philippines, Poland, Portugal, Puerto Rico, Romania, Senegal, South Africa, Spain, Sweden, Switzerland, Thailand, United States, Uruguay, Venezuela, Vietnam and Yugoslavia.

If you would like further information about International PEN's activities please contact:

Alexander Blokh, International Secretary,
International PEN Headquarters,
38 King St, London WC2E 8JT (01-379-6353).